To Radvin, Mahya, and Fatemeh:
Understanding cultures is a way of getting in touch with the complexity of human beings.

Title: Yalda: Celebration of the Longest Night
Summery: A grandma is explaining Yalda night to her grandchildren
Author: Nafiseh Jahanbakht
Illustrator: Elham Eslami Eshlagi

@Nafiseh Jahanbakht, 2024
All rights reserved

ISBN: 9798345839782
Imprint: Independently published

Grandma is preparing the house for the Yalda celebration.

Mahya and Radvin went to help their grandma.

"Granny! Can you explain about Yalda night?" asked Radvin.

"And why would we eat watermelon on Yalda?" Mahya wondered.

THE PERSIAN EMPIRE ABOUT 500 B.C.

"Oh my dearest! Let me tell you all about it." Grandma said with a smile. "Long time ago, people who were living in Persia were mostly farmers. The sunlight was important to them. Can you guess why?"

"Is it because there was no electricity back then?" Radvin asked.

"Absolutely!" Grandma nodded. "In the old times, natural light from sun was crucial in people's lives, especially for farmers. Tasks like planting, harvesting, and tending to animals could only be done when the sunlight was available."

Many years ago, Persians discovered that the last day of Fall marks the longest night of the year. They decided to celebrate this special night with gatherings and festivities. This celebration is called Shab-e Yalda, which means 'The Night of the Sun's Birth'. After Yalda night, the days gradually begin to grow longer, symbolizing the return of light and warmth.

Also, the official calendar of the Persian Empire from more than 2500 years ago, recognized Yalda night. So, as you see, Yalda has been known among Persians for a long time. Surely, it has its own traditions.

In the past, Persians would save some summer fruits for winter. They believed that fruits and nuts would keep them healthy and strong against winter diseases. So, the first tradition is to eat seasonal fruits and nuts.

Pomegranates and watermelons are especially significant on Yalda night because of their red color. They symbolize the crimson hues of dawn and the glow of life.

"Grandma! Are you going
to read us stories tonight?"
Mahya asked. "Yes! I'm
going to tell you the story
of the Phoenix or Simorgh."
Grandma responded.

"I'd love to hear the story! Is it magical?" Mahya asked. Her eyes were shining with excitement. "Kind of magical!" Grandma nodded. "In Persian stories, Simorgh is a mythical bird with healing powers and immense wisdom."

"Should we set up the table now?" said Radvin excitedly.

"Yes! We need our fruits and nuts on the table."

"Can you also bring the fruit bowl with persimmons?" Grandma asked Mahya. "Persimmons are very healthy with lots of vitamins" She added.

"I also made some Baklava that we
can add to our table." said grandma
while bringing a plate full of Baklava.

"What else do we need Granny?" inquired Radvin.
"We can also put candles that symbolize the victory
of light over darkness" replied Grandma.

"Now, we just need to add a book of poetry." Said Grandma while bringing the book.
"The rhythms of poetry enriches our celebration and adds to the joy of this night. For tonight, I'd like to add a book by Rumi who was a famous Persian poet." she added.

MEVLANA CELALEDDIN RUMI

"Rumi made poems?" Radvin asked.

"Yes. He was a very wise man. He put some of his teachings in poems with symbolic stories. His poems are a little like Yalda Night – they bring people together to share wisdom and happiness, even when times are dark." Grandma explained.

"In this earth,
in this soil,
in this pure field,
let's not plant any seed
other than seeds of
Compassion and Love."
                    -Rumi

Yalda night carries deep symbolic meanings for Persians. It is an ancient festival for celebrating the longest night of the year. This celebration has been observed for thousands of years. It is a celebration that not only marks a natural phenomenon but also reinforces cultural values and family unity.

HAPPY YALDA NIGHT

HAPPY
YALDA NIGHT

Can you name these fruits?

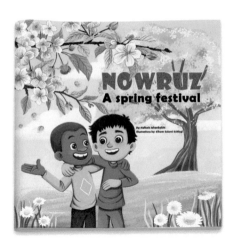

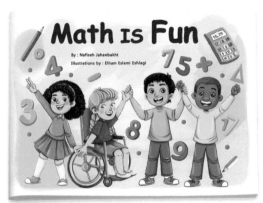

About the illustrator

Elham is an illustrator
who works with
vibrant colors and
creates visually stunning illustrations for kids.
Her work has depth, vibrancy, and ability to bring
stories to life.

elina.es26@gmail.com

About the Author

Nafiseh, a math
educator and college
professor, is a parent
of an amazing boy who loves math and is interested
in persian culture.

Made in United States
Troutdale, OR
12/09/2024